We Bought a Zoo
幸せへのキセキ

編著者

◆

森岡裕一
沖野泰子
白木智士
山科美和子
横山三鶴

英宝社

音声ファイルのダウンロード方法

英宝社ホームページ（http://www.eihosha.co.jp/）の
「テキスト音声ダウンロード」バナーをクリックすると、
音声ファイルダウンロードページにアクセスできます。

はじめに

English without tears. なる言い回しがあるが、もしそれが何らの苦労なく英語を習得できるという意味なら、それはありえない。だが、もし、楽しく英語を学習するということなら、それは十分可能であって、そのひとつが面白い映画を楽しみながら、ついでに、そこで使われている英語を体得するという方法だ。

そんな思いで、編著者たちは17年前に、『ミュージック・オブ・ハート』という教科書を作製した。有り難いことに、そのテキストは好評を博すことができた。映画が優れていたことにくわえ、映画をつまみ食いすることなく、さまざまな演習を通して、自然にスクリプトのほぼ全容がたどれるよう工夫したことがよかったのかもしれない。

今回、メンバーが再結集し（一部、新メンバー）、新たな題材で、いっそう使い勝手のいい教材を開発した結果が本書である。前回は格差と教育がテーマであったが、今回のテーマは人と動物の交流、家族愛である。ペットブームの陰に、多くの動物が殺処分されたり虐待される昨今、時宜にかなったテーマだと思う。

基本的な編集方針は前回と同様であるが、ポイントを列挙しておきたい。

1. 題材のレベルでいうと、本書は中級レベルであってけっして易しくはないが、設問や様々なヒントによって、誰もがとっつきやすく感じられるよう工夫した。Pre-Viewing セクションを充実させ、映画鑑賞に必要な語彙や知識などが自然に身につくよう努力した。

2. 音声に関しては、英語音声学の理論に基づいたきわめて実践的なアドバイスが付されている。あえて網羅的であることを目指すより、簡潔にして要を押さえた本書の Tips がどれほど有効かは、学習を終えたときに実感されるはずだと自負している。

3. 関連する英文記事をはさんで、学習にメリハリをつけるよう考慮した。映画と原作の違いなどにふれ、映画から始めて原作を読んでみたいと思う学生が現れれば幸いである。あわせて、写真などもふんだんに盛り込み、映画の雰囲気が伝わるよう最大限の努力をおこなった。

4. 本書は全 12 のユニットに英文の読み物やイントロダクションをくわえ、半期 15 回の使用に耐えられるよう構成されている。「学生も教師も使いやすい」教科書を作るという精神を忘れることなく、TM、付録の DVD など資料を充実させている。

5.上記の目的を果たすため、本書の編集チームはさまざまな背景をもつ5人で作られている。編著者たちは、英米文学、英語音声学、英語教育学の専門家として研究するかたわら、長年、各地で英語教育を実践する立場にある。日々体験する問題などを情報交換しながら、使いやすく楽しいテキストを作るべく、それぞれの立場から貢献したチームワークの成果が本書である。

なお、本書をさらに充実させるために、現場で実際にご使用いただいた先生方から、ご批判、ご意見をお寄せいただければ、編著者たちとしてはこれに過ぎる喜びはない。

最後になったが、本テキストの方針に賛同し、出版を勧めてくださった英宝社社長佐々木元氏、編集の下村幸一氏はじめ英宝社のみなさまに謝意を表しておきたい。

森岡裕一、沖野泰子、白木智士、山科美和子、横山三鶴

（ABC 順）

Contents

Introduction

みなさま、*We Bought a Zoo* の世界へようこそ。この物語は実話に基づいた物語ですが、もちろん舞台設定など実話とは異なる部分があります。この話はのちの Reading Recess に譲りましょう。主な登場人物（もの）は Benjamin Mee とその家族、そして動物園の従業員、それから動物たちです。映画の魅力の一つは何と言っても、動く実物が見られることではないでしょうか。この映画でも、日常生活では目にすることのない動物たちがスクリーンで動き回ります。そこで、この Introduction ではまずは映画に登場する人ではなく、動物について少し確認をしてから各ユニットに入りたいと思います。

写真にあてはまる動物名とその動物にあてはまる説明の記号を選択肢から選んでみましょう。

動物名

buffalo	camel	capuchin	giraffe	grizzly bear	hawk	jaguar
kangaroo	lemur	lion	llama	otter	owl	peafowl
snake	porcupine	tiger	tortoise	wild boar	zebra	

説　明

a) a large wild bird that eats small birds and animals
b) a very large strong animal with thick brown fur that eats flesh, fruit, and insects. They live in the Northwest of North America
c) a slow-moving land animal that can pull its head and legs into the hard round shell that covers its body
d) a large bird, the male of which has long shiny blue and green tail feathers that it can lift up and spread out
e) a large desert animal with a long neck and one or two humps (= large raised parts) on its back
f) a large South American wild cat with brown and yellow fur and black spots
g) a large strong animal that is orange with black lines on its body and is a member of the cat family
h) an animal that looks like a horse, but has black and white lines all over its body
i) a large animal of the cat family that lives in Africa and parts of southern Asia. They have gold-colored fur and the male has a mane (= hair around his neck)
j) an Australian animal that has strong back legs for jumping and carries its babies in a pouch (= a special pocket of skin) on its stomach
k) an animal with long sharp needle-like parts growing all over its back and sides.
l) a South American animal with thick hair like wool and a long neck
m) an African animal similar to a large black cow with long curved horns
n) a small animal like a monkey with large eyes and a long tail, that lives mainly in Madagascar
o) a bird that hunts at night and has a large head, eyes that face forward, and a loud call
p) a large wild pig with long hair
q) a tall African animal with a very long neck and legs and dark spots on its yellow-brown fur
r) a small animal that can swim, has brown fur, and eats fish
s) an animal with a long thin body and no legs, that often has a poisonous bite
t) a small animal with a long tail, which uses its hands to climb trees and is found in tropical forests from Nicaragua to Paraguay

Unit 1 公親業の苦労

I. Pre-Viewing

CD 1

A Words

Choose the appropriate word from the list below.

1. I want you to have eggs, because you need the ( ).
2. Read the label carefully to make sure that they are ( ) free.
3. ( ) slippers are on your feet.
4. You're gonna get an ( ), if you don't work hard.
5. Only ( ) people ridicule a kid whose mom died six months ago.
6. Nasty people often cause ( ) harm or damage.
7. The girl we met at Jamba Juice was a ( ).
8. It looks like his shop is closed for ( ).
9. I assure you that human ( ) is a good thing.
10. ( ) to start over and let a little sunlight in.

attempt	F	gluten	insidious	interaction
pernicious	protein	reindeer	renovations	stunner

Phrases

Study the following phrases.

1. Come on. We are late, guys.
2. "Whatever" is the laziest word of the 20th century, so it is over.
3. This lasagna makes dinner for three.
4. I'll get the dish back to you in time.
5. That actually means Bernie's hung over.
6. Will you just do me a favor?

Notes

gonna=going to	**Jamba Juice**=famous juice joint

妻に先立たれたベンジャミンは長男ディランと長女ロージーの朝食の準備、学校への送迎などで毎日忙しい生活を送ります。一方、兄のダンカンはベンジャミンに愛妻の死を乗り越えて新しい人生を始めろと助言します。

II. First Viewing

Watch the film and decide if each statement is true (T) or false(F). If you choose F, explain what is wrong.

1. Today they got up early, so there is enough time for school. ( )
2. The children always say good morning to their father. ( )
3. Some woman invites Benjamin to go hiking by telephone. ( )
4. Benjamin doesn't like the way Dylan replies to him. ( )
5. Benjamin thinks Dylan focuses on his homework as much as on his artwork. ( )
6. A woman offers some cakes as dessert for today's dinner. ( )
7. Little Dom's is closed for renovations. ( )
8. It is likely that the brothers will not have lunch together soon. ( )

III. Second Viewing

Watch the film again, then select the correct answer.

1. Why is Dylan so concerned with the label of the food?

   a) Because it is expensive.
   b) Because it is not his favorite brand.
   c) Because he can't eat it, unless it is gluten free.

2. What is The Seventh Tower likely to be?

   a) Dylan's artwork
   b) Dylan's homework
   c) Dylan's video game

3. What can you infer from the woman's statement, "Or four"?

a) She wants to be invited to dinner.
b) She wants the family to eat enough.
c) She doesn't like lasagna herself.

4. Why did Ben and Duncan have trouble finding a place to have lunch?

a) Most of the restaurants are closed.
b) Ben doesn't like to go to the places where he and his wife used to go.
c) They are all gluten free restaurants.

5. What did Duncan do to find himself?

a) He looked for an ideal woman at Jamba Juice.
b) He tried to ascertain that human interaction was a good thing.
c) He spent half a year on a commercial fishing boat.

Ⅳ. Dictation

CD 3

Listen to the CD and fill in the blanks.

Ben: All right, McGinty, so ①______________ .
I go to the volcano eruption ②__________ .
And I take the kids.
And I write about the end of the ③____________ from the point of view of the generation that's gonna save it.
And we do a whole thing about how life is ④______________ , and all the software, and laptops, and apps in the world aren't gonna ⑤________________ . And we call it... You ready?
iPocalypse.

Boss: Wow. Just wow.

Ben: ⑥______________ , right?
I mean, I think ⑦______________ be a series, like the killer bees.

Boss: That is bold stuff.

Ben: You're not gonna say yes, are you?

Boss: No. Listen.

I think we should give you an online column.

That way, you'll be ⑧__________________ .

This is the way we live now.

If the paper goes down or gets ⑨__________ , you'll still be safe.

You'll be viral.

Ben: ⑩________________ me around out of...

Boss: I am not!

Listening Tip ◆ 破裂音 + 子音 / 無音

単語の末尾が破裂音で次に母音が来ない場合、破裂音が聞こえにくくなります。

1. He is Bob [ボ(ブ)].
2. Don't [ドン(ト)] go.
3. I like [ライ(ク)] that [ザッ(ト)].

単語の中でも起こります。

4. cupboard [カッ( )ボード] (この単語の場合は本当に“プ”が発音されません)

V. Post-Viewing

映画の冒頭部分をもう一度見て、ベンジャミン・ミーの過去の経歴を整理してみましょう。

ベンジャミンは冒険ルポライターで、数々の危険な場所に身を置いたことがある。

経歴1→ 防護服を着て [ ]

経歴2→ [ ] にインタビューを試み、
[ ] をしてその場をなごませた。

経歴3→ ヘリコプターで [ ]

最後の台詞はどういう意味かを推測してみましょう。

But nothing prepared him for this one.

コ・ラ・ム 「デイモン vs ヨハンソン」

この映画の主要人物の二人、ベンジャミン・ミーとケリー・フォスターを演じた役者について一瞥しておこう。まず、ベンジャミン役のマット・デイモン。1970 年マサチューセッツ州生まれのアメリカ人男優である。小さいころから役者をめざし、ハーヴァード大学在学中に端役ながら映画・テレビに出演している。彼が成功を収めるきっかけは幼馴染のベン・アフレックとともに書いた脚本が、1998 年『グッドウイル・ハンティング / 旅立ち』として映画化され、アフレックとともにアカデミー脚本賞を受賞、主演男優賞にノミネートされたことによる。その後、『プライベート・ライアン』(1998)、『リプリー』(1999)、『オーシャンズ 11』(2001) などに出演するが、なんといっても彼の名を高めたのが、その後続編が 4 本製作されることになる、アクションスリラー『ボーン・アイデンティティ』(2002) である。記憶を失ったスパイに迫る数々の危機と、彼の屈折した心理描写が上質のエンターテインメントに仕上がって大成功を収めている。デイモンは『オーシャンズ』シリーズとともにアクションものが多いが、シリアスなドラマも少なくない。たとえば、クリント・イーストウッド監督のアパルトヘイトとラグビーを主題にした『インビクタス / 負けざるものたち』(2009) の熱演では、アカデミー助演男優賞、ゴールデングローブ助演男優賞にノミネートされている。その後、本作『幸せへのキセキ』(2011)、火星に一人取り残された宇宙飛行士を演じた『オデッセイ』(2015) など、多様な役柄を演じている。

いっぽう、ケリー役のスカーレット・ヨハンソンは、1984 年生まれのデンマーク系アメリカ人だ。幼いころから演劇学校に通い、10 歳前後にいくつかの映画賞でノミネートされるほど早熟だった。彼女が注目されたのは東京、京都を舞台にした大人の淡いラブロマンス『ロスト・イン・トランスレーション』(2003)、同年のフェルメールの絵画をモチーフにした『真珠の耳飾りの少女』で、前者は英国アカデミー主演女優賞、ゴールデングローブ主演女優賞ノミネート、後者は両方でノミネートされている。その後、「アベンジャーズ」シリーズなど、けっして作品に恵まれているとは言い難いが、本作や『ブラック・ダリア』(2006)、『それでも恋するバルセロナ』(2008)、『ヒッチコック』(2012) などで、印象的な演技を披露している。また、彼女はチャリティ活動や中絶推進団体を支持するなど政治的にも積極的で、強い女のイメージは本作でも十分発揮されている。

Unit 2 心機一転

I. Pre-Viewing

A Words

Choose the appropriate word from the list below.

1. It was kind of their (   ) since they left the cashbox on the counter.
2. He has received three (   ) in one semester.
3. What is that noise? It is so (   ) .
4. I need to fix my (   ) window.
5. Besides today's (   ), there is a darkness that we need to deal with.
6. We (   ) creativity at the school.
7. Although Bob Marley was a great singer, we don't (   ) all that he stood for.
8. I'm sorry but we have to (   ) Dylan.
9. I'm looking for a house with a (   ) backyard.
10. My (   ) go out to you and your family.

annoying	condolences	encourage	endorse	expel
fault	squeaky	substantial	suspensions	theft

B Phrases

Study the following phrases.

1. Dad, stop. Here he comes.
2. You stole! It breaks my heart.
3. I'm gonna take baldness off my list of things to worry about.
4. The more, the merrier.
5. We are now running out of options.

Notes

mural: 壁画
Bob Marley: (1945 - 1981) ジャマイカ出身の有名なレゲエミュージシャン
Charles Manson: (1934 - 2017) 米国のカルト指導者、犯罪者

ティーンエージャーの息子ディランは母を失った悲しみを乗り越えられず、校則違反を繰り返します。一方、幼いロージーは夜に寝付けないでいます。家族の心機一転を図るため、ベンジャミンは愛妻との思い出が詰まった街から引っ越すことを決心し、新居探しを始めます。

II. First Viewing

Watch the film and decide if each statement is true (T) or false(F). If you choose F, explain what is wrong.

1. Dylan seems to reflect on himself and regret his conduct. ( )
2. The teacher is worried about Dylan's mental health. ( )
3. The school expels Dylan for his artwork. ( )
4. Rosie thinks her father is better looking than the other fathers. ( )
5. Rosie has trouble sleeping because the neighbors' music is too loud. ( )
6. According to the realtor, more people want to buy than to sell in the current housing market. ( )
7. Benjamin thinks the realtor is a strange man. ( )
8. The realtor has been doing his job for a long time. ( )

III. Second Viewing

Watch the film again, then select the correct answer.

• Section 1

1. How many times has Dylan been suspended in this semester so far?

   a) two　　b) three　　c) four

2. How would you describe Dylan's drawing on the wall?

   a) creative and whimsical
   b) nice and colorful
   c) dark and violent

3. What has broken Benjamin's heart most?

a) Dylan's artwork
b) Dylan's theft
c) Dylan's school grade

• Section 2

4. What is Rosie making in the kitchen?

a) a snack after dinner
b) lasagna for dinner
c) a peanut butter and jelly sandwich for lunch

5. How often does Rosie have trouble falling asleep?

a) rarely
b) sometimes
c) every night

• Section 3

6. What kind of house is Benjamin looking for?

a) a house with a huge backyard
b) a new house in the city
c) a house on the hills

7. Rosie says to Benjamin, "I know, but he should have!" She means that...

a) Dylan should have come with them.
b) the realtor should have found a new house.
c) the realtor should have known her mother.

8. How many houses does the realtor show to Benjamin and Rosie?

a) one
b) a couple of them
c) many

Ⅳ. Dictation

Listen to the CD and fill in the blanks.

Benjamin: Classy... Real classy.
Dylan: They left the cashbox right on the counter. ①________________ kind of their fault if you think about it.

Benjamin: That's three suspensions in ②______________. That's gotta be ③______________ record.

Dylan: Yeah, well, maybe ④______________ a prize.

Benjamin: Could you possibly be making a joke right now? Jesus, ⑤______________ annoying!

Dylan: Dad, stop.

Benjamin: No, ⑥______________ fix it.

Dylan: Dad, here he come...

Benjamin: Frame's a little loose.

Principal: I...

Benjamin: Just give me one second.

Principal: ⑦______________ fine with my squeaky window, Mr. Mee. In fact, I rather enjoy it. Besides today's theft, there's a darkness here that we need to ⑧______________. Mr. Devereaux, Dylan's art teacher, wanted you to see his wall mural. We encourage creativity at the school. There's a nice treatment of the word "love". A whimsical portraiture of recycling. A hard-hitting exposé about world peace. Here is the great Bob Marley. Though we don't endorse all that he stood for. Sunflowers. And ⑨______________ which one is your son's. We're a three-strike school, Mr. Mee, and today was his fourth strike. I'm sorry. We have to expel Dylan. But, as one parent to another, I... I would examine his ⑩______________ life.

Listening Tip ◆ 聞こえなくなる代名詞

代名詞、特に it や I 等の母音で始まるものはほとんどの場合アクセントを持たないため曖昧な音になります。それに加えて文頭の単語は強く発音しにくいため脱落して聞こえなくなることがあります。

(例)

1. I [(ア)イもしくは無音の(アィ)] don't like it.
2. He [(ヒ)イ] calls you.

V. Post-Viewing

Unit 2 内の学校に関連する英語表現を整理してみましょう。

1. That's three suspensions in one semester.
2. We're a three-strike school, and today was his fourth strike.
3. He expelled you because you stole.

その他の学校に関連する表現も確認してみましょう。

4. The teacher called on me to answer the question.
5. My exam results were poor, but I passed the class.
6. I often take notes on the lecture.
7. Why did you skip school yesterday?
8. I need six more credits in order to graduate.
9. Don't be tardy for school.

Unit 3「動物園買っちゃった」

I. Pre-Viewing

A Words

Choose the appropriate word from the list below.

1. What is so ( ) about this place?
2. I would like to buy the property and then ( ) the animals.
3. I almost blew Dad's ( ) by buying a broken-down zoo.
4. Running the zoo is my ( ).
5. The zoo makes 75% of its ( ) in the summertime.
6. If I can get an ( ) set for the end of June, I'll be open by July.
7. There are 47 species, seven of which are ( ).
8. The kids are going to be so ( ).
9. Benjamin is going to ( ) his children.
10. The sweatshirt started out as mine, but she ( ) it.

adopted	complicated	destiny	endangered	home-school(v)
inheritance	inspection	psyched	relocate	revenue

B Phrases

Study the following phrases.

1. I think we're jumpin' the gun.
2. The estate's been maintaining the zoo for now, just to keep it up.
3. Once you see what it is, then you can figure it out.
4. I'm beggin' you, do what other people do.
5. Let that sweatshirt start over.

Notes

stipulation: 条項、規定　　**Target**: 米国の大手スーパーマーケットチェーン

不動産業者が最後に仕方なく案内したワケ有り物件にロージーは大興奮します。劇的に変わってしまう生活を選択しようとしているベンジャミンに、兄ダンカンや息子ディランは猛反対します。ベンジャミンたちの新生活はどうなるのでしょうか。

II. First Viewing

Watch the film and decide if each statement is true (T) or false(F). If you choose F, explain what is wrong.

1. At first sight Benjamin is pleased with the Rosemoor property. ( )
2. The realtor strongly recommends the Rosemoor property. ( )
3. If Benjamin buys the property, he must promise to keep the endangered animals. ( )
4. If no one buys the property, the animals will probably have to be deserted. ( )
5. Duncan agrees with Benjamin's plan to buy the property with a zoo. ( )
6. Duncan himself went through a difficult time when his wife left him. ( )
7. Both Rosie and Dylan are excited about moving to a new place in the country. ( )
8. The neon sign at the restaurant says, "WELCOME BRAVE NEW OWNERS." ( )

III. Second Viewing

Watch the film again, and write the name of the speaker (Realtor, Benjamin, Rosie, Duncan, Dylan). Then watch the film again and put the sentences into the right order.

• Section 1

1. "The Rosemoor property has some challenges." (Realtor)[1]
2. "Don't take a gift that's not given to you yet." ( )[ ]
3. "I'm gonna live here. I'm gonna keep you." ( )[ ]

4. “You don’t have to take a picture.” ( )[ ]

5. “I don’t know anything about animals and zoos.” ( )[ ]

6. “This was a fully functioning zoo until two years ago.” ( )[ ]

7. “What’s so complicated about this place?” ( )[ ]

• Section 2

1. “This is what happens when people have a you-know-what occur in their lives.” (Duncan)[1]

2. “The place makes 75% of its revenue in the summertime.” ( )[ ]

3. “Monmmy used to wear this sometimes.” ( )[ ]

4. “This is what you want. It’s not what I want” ( )[ ]

5. “Go to Vegas. Lose a little bit of money..” ( )[ ]

6. “The kids are gonna be so psyched.” ( )[ ]

7. “My friends are here! Our life is here!” ( )[ ]

Ⅳ. Dictation

CD 11

Listen to the CD and fill in the blanks.

Benjamin: ①______________, let’s let this shirt start over! Okay, ②______________ left. A good one. Oldie but a goodie. ③______________ do you think?

Rosie: Mommy used to ④______________ that sometimes.

Benjamin: She did. This was a... It ⑤______________ as mine, but she kind of adopted it. But it’s got rips and everything everywhere. Tough to ⑥______________ some of these things ⑦______________, right? ⑧______________ ?

Rosie: ⑨______________. Let that sweatshirt start over.

Benjamin: Let it start over. Okay. This is it. Last item.

Rosie: ⑩______________. That, we're keeping!

Benjamin: Okay.

Listing Tip ◆「母音＋[r]」のこもった音

アメリカ発音では、「母音 + [r]」は、二つの音ではなく一つの「母音のこもった音」になってしまうので、[r] が聞こえなくなります。「こもった音」とは舌先を上もしくは口の奥に向けて舌にくぼみを作り、空気の流れを滞らせてできる音です。母音が後についた [r] は日本語のラ行のように聞こえるので聞き取りに問題はありません。しかし文末のため後に音が続かない場合や子音が後に続いた場合は母音の音色が変化するのみなので聞き取りが難しいのです。

（例）

1. It is in the car. [カー]（注：「ー」の部分がこもってます）
2. It is in the car at [カーラット] the park [パーク].

V. Post-Viewing

不動産業者はベンジャミンが早まった決断をしないよう様々な表現で落ち着かせようとします。それらを整理してみましょう。

1. Let's not rush into things.
2. I think we're jumpin' the gun.
3. Let's not get ahead of ourselves.
4. Let's just take it all in first.
5. Don't take a gift that's not given to you yet.

上記の表現を使ってペアで会話してみましょう。

例 A: I think Benjamin's jumpin' the gun.
B: No, I don't think so. That is exactly what he's been looking for.

Unit 4 スタッフと動物たち

I. Pre-Viewing

A Words

Choose the appropriate word from the list below.

1. He built the (   ) that set the standards for modern zoos all across America.
2. Lily is 13 and she can't (   ) work here.
3. I would like to (   ) us all modern-day adventurers.
4. There are a couple of things I need to go over with you about the (   ) inspection.
5. Buster has been stressed out and he is occasionally (   ).
6. Tigers and lions are very different. Tigers don't (   ) like lions.
7. When tigers attack, they bite you and take your (   ) with their teeth.
8. We need to have Spar seen by the large animal (   ) from San Diego.
9. He is a (   ) guy from the city. No one in the zoo community knows him.
10. I'm here every day and shoveling bear shit. I'm (   )!

declare	depressed	enclosures	legally	pathetic
pulse	random	roar	upcoming	vet

B Phrases

Study the following phrases.

1. We pay her cash <u>under the table</u> out of my salary.
2. Buster can <u>rip</u> your arm <u>off</u>.
3. Jaguars and tigers don't <u>get along</u>.
4. We need somebody who can really <u>take charge of</u> this place.
5. You did a good job. <u>Well done</u>!

Notes

capuchin: オマキザル
USDA=United States Department of Agriculture 米国農務省
grizzly (grizzly bear): グリズリー、ハイイログマ
Paxil: うつ病と不安障害の治療薬　**meds**=medications
canines=canine teeth 犬歯　**aorta**: 大動脈　**carotid**: 頸動脈

引っ越しを終えたベンジャミンたちが動物園のスタッフや動物たちとの初顔合わせをする日がやってきます。経済的な問題を抱えた動物園の実情を改めて知ったベンジャミンですが、それらにどのように対応していくのでしょうか。

II. First Viewing

Watch the film and decide if each statement is true (T) or false(F). If you choose F, explain what is wrong.

1. Peter and Robin take care of everything in the zoo including bookkeeping. (　)
2. Lily is Kelly's daughter who lives on the property. (　)
3. They don't have enough money to pay Buster's medicine. (　)
4. Tigers have sensors in front of their canines and can detect the pulse with them. (　)
5. If they ask a large animal vet to come to the zoo, it's going to cost a lot. (　)
6. The word cages instead of enclosures has been used for a long time. (　)
7. Kelly is wondering if the new owner is serious about keeping the zoo. (　)
8. Peter feels bitter about Walter Ferris because Walter stole his wife. (　)

III. Second Viewing

• Section 1

Watch the film again, identify these people and animals, and choose the appropriate description.

Kelly	is a (1) zookeeper.
Robin	is a (2).
Peter	is their (3) and built the (4).
Rhonda	is in charge of (5).
Lily	works at the Jaguar (6).
Nathan	takes care of (7) and (8).
Buster	is a North American grizzly (9).
Spar	is a 17-year-old Bengal (10).

bear	bookkeeping	craftsman	enclosures	feeding
head	restaurant	tiger	visionary	watering

• Section 2

Answer with as many adjectives as you can which describe Kelly.

Ⅳ. Dictation

Listen to the CD and fill in the blanks.

Rosie: I thought they would roar like Solomon ①_____________ .

Kelly: No, ②_____________ and lions are very different. Tigers don't ③_____________ or roar, they chuff. Like...

(Kelly makes a chuff sound and Rosie does, too.)

Kelly: Yeah. When you chuff at them, they ④_____________ , see? Try, ⑤_____________ .

Dylan: Oh, my God.

Kelly: That guy ⑥_____________ , that's Spar. He's ⑦_____________ . He's 17. He's a Bengal tiger. You know, tigers have ⑧_____________ sensors in the front of their two-inch canines. They can ⑨_____________ detect the pulse in your aorta. So when ⑩_____________ , they bite you, take your pulse with their teeth, reposition those suckers and boom, there goes your carotid.

Dylan: Wow.

Kelly: Yeah.

Listening Tip◆[l] の音

日本語にない音である [l] は、舌先だけを前歯の直後につけて出す音で、「くぐもったウ」に聞こえます。次に母音が来ない場合は前の母音と区別することが難しくなります。母音が後続する際は、後続する母音とつながって日本語のラ行の様な音が出ます。

(例)

1. L. [エウ]
2. All [オーウ] right.
3. The light [ライト] is on the ceiling [シーリング].

V. Post-Viewing

A Unit 4 の最後の場面（仕事を終えて Jaguar restaurant で楽しんでいるシーン）を再度観て、答えましょう。ピーターが USDA の検査官ウォルター・フェリスをひどく憎んでいるのは何故でしょう。

[①] 年代に [②] が [③] を盗んだ。[④] の様々なアイディアを盗み、それらを他の動物園に売り渡した。そのアイディアは動物園の [⑤] や堀に関するものだった。そのせいで Rosemoor Wildlife Park は [⑥]。

B 次の台詞はどういう意味かペアで互いに説明してみましょう。

1. Kelly の "My brief marriage; that was a cage."

____

____

2. Nathan の "He'll never last."

____

____

コ・ラ・ム 「アメリカの味」

この映画の中に「アメリカらしい」食べ物がよく登場しているのに気づいただろうか。まず、lasagna（ラザニア）である。アメリカの「おふくろの味」とされるラザニアは家庭料理の定番と言えるだろう。ロージーの友人のママたちは手作りしたラザニアを競うようにベンジャミンに差し入れし、「家庭的な女性」をアピールしている。一方、ベンジャミンはそれらを冷蔵庫に入れっぱなしで、全く興味を示さない。

次に、夕食後のキッチンでロージーが peanut butter and jelly sandwich（ピーナッツバター&ジェリー・サンドイッチ）を作っているシーンがある。アメリカの子どもたちが学校へ持って行くランチとして代表的なものの1つで、薄切り食パンの片面にピーナッツバター、もう１枚にジェリー（果肉を含まないジャムのようなもの）を塗って合わせただけのシンプルなサンドイッチだ。幼いロージーは健気にもママ役を務めようと奮闘している。

さらに、ベンジャミンの妻が大好きだったスイーツの1つとして Pop Tarts（ポップ・ターツ / タルト）が出てくる。タルト生地の中央にフルーツジャムやチョコレートが挟まっているもので、アメリカではシリアルと同様に朝食やおやつとして一般的である。ブルーベリー味やストロベリー味など様々あるが、次々に新フレーバーが発売されるほど人気が高い。Frosted タイプは、甘い砂糖のペーストが塗られており、カラフルでポップなデザイン付きである。トースターや電子レンジで少し温めると、アメリカ特有の激甘のスイーツが出来上がる。

Unit 5 新生活はいかに？

I. Pre-Viewing

A Words

Choose the appropriate word from the list below.

1. These animals aren't ( ) at night.
2. You're drilling yourself into ( ) debt.
3. Okay. Here's the ( ) Duncan plan.
4. You should ( ) the animals and keep Kelly.
5. I'm trying to give them an ( ) American experience.
6. I slipped on the roof and ( ) my nose.
7. Benjamin bought a ( ) house in the countryside.
8. There is a new ( ) of exotic snakes in the garage.
9. I'll put those snakes in the ( ) in the morning.
10. It's nine point two miles each way, so ( ), that's 18.4 miles for butter.

authentic	banged	docile	dump (v)	exhibit
insane	revised	shipment	technically	weird

B Phrases

Study the following phrases.

1. Now you're talking to them. There you go.
2. At the risk of stating the obvious, you're silly.
3. We're gonna take a vote.
4. Do you think butter is worth your dad driving 18 miles to get it?
5. Make sure the lights are off in the side room. Get it done!
6. Do you remember the night that we were tucking you in?

Notes

asshole: ばか野郎　　**veloured**: ベロア調の
a Chilean miner: 2010年チリで起きた鉱山崩落事故で、69日後に全員救出された炭鉱夫を指す

翌朝、ベンジャミンは杭打ちなど動物園の改修作業を開始します。兄ダンカンは経済的な厳しさから、何とか諦めるよう説得を続けます。ベンジャミンは新オーナーとして上手くやっていけるのでしょうか。

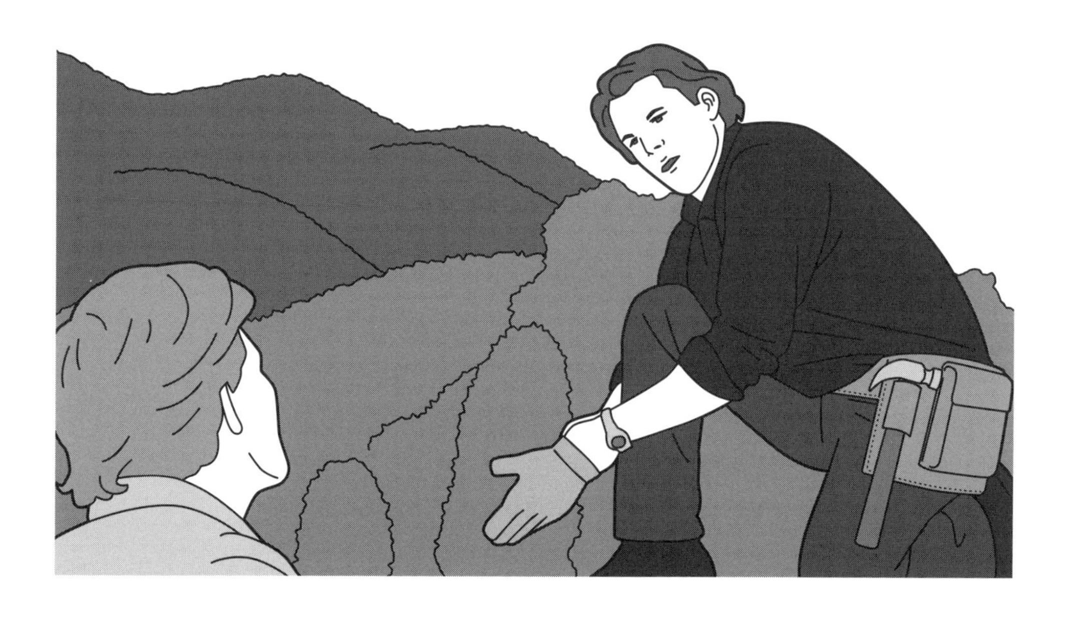

II. First Viewing

Watch the film and decide if each statement is true (T) or false(F). If you choose F, explain what is wrong.

1. Duncan is worried about Benjamin financially. ( )
2. Lily is interested in Dylan and his drawings. ( )
3. Rhonda points out that there is not enough money in the zoo. ( )
4. Dylan and Rosie make Benjamin drive 80 miles just to get butter. ( )
5. They put a box full of snakes in the garage which Kelly is going to take care of in the following morning. ( )
6. Kelly finishes her work for the day, so she is going out to the city with her girlfriend. ( )
7. Rosie is upset because her friends don't visit her in the new place. ( )
8. Benjamin realizes Rosie is trying to be happy but misses her mother a lot. ( )

III. Second Viewing

Watch the film again, and answer the following questions.

• Section 1

1. What kind of future does Duncan predict if Benjamin keeps working in the zoo?

____

____

2. What does Lily promise to do for Dylan every day?

____

• Section 2

3. How far is it from the zoo to the nearest grocery store?

____

4. After Kelly leaves, what does Benjamin have to do that night?

To give Spar [   ].

To [   ] in the garage.

To leave a new shipment of [   ] in the crates.

To give the monkeys [   ].

• Section 3

5. Benjamin finds something in Rosie's bed and he calls it "our old friend." What is it?

____

____

6. Before Rosie's mother passed away, what did she say to ease Rosie's mind?

____

____

Ⅳ. Dictation

Listen to the CD and fill in the blanks.

Benjamin: Now what do we have here? It's our old friend. I didn't think this one was gonna make the trip.

Rosie: Did Mama hurt a lot before she had to ①______________ us?

Benjamin: Well... Well, do ②______________ the night that we were tucking you in, and you asked Mommy that? No?

Rosie: No.

Benjamin: Well, she said... She said that ③______________ worse than ④______________. Remember? She said sometimes people look really sick but they don't feel really sick. Do you feel like you can't ⑤______________ ?

Rosie: Yeah.

Benjamin: And you feel like you can't hear ⑥______________ ?

Rosie: Uh-huh.

Rosie: But I know what to do. Catch ⑦______________.

Benjamin: Catch her spirit. That's right.

Rosie: Here it comes.

Benjamin: Okay, look for it. There you go. And ⑧______________ in your heart. It fell. Okay, get it. Hold it there. Can you see her?

Rosie: Yeah.

Benjamin: Yeah? ⑨______________ never far away.

Rosie: Right there.

Benjamin: That's right. Mommy would always be in your heart and my ⑩____________. Are you ready to go to bed? Do you want to... Do you want to keep this? Okay. Okay, sweetheart. Good night.

Listening Tip ◆ 消える [h] の音

[h] で始まる所有格と目的格の代名詞 his、him、her は前の動詞や前置詞と続けて発音されると h が落ちて、それぞれ「イズ」、「イム」、「ア」になります。her の [h] が落ちた発音は [r] の入った「こもったア」です。

（例）

1. I caught him [コートイム].　　2. Take her [テイクア] with you.

V. Post-Viewing

A 話し言葉の短縮形を書き言葉に換えて意味を確認しましょう。

1. You're gonna love your new enclosure.
→
2. You gotta be real with 'em. →
3. What ya doin'? →
4. You gotta take your meds. →
5. He's gonna be okay. →

B 上記 A を参考にして、短縮形の表現を声に出して言ってみましょう。

1. 私はここに住むのよ。
2. 多数決にしよう。
3. 彼女は家に帰らないと。
4. どこへ行くの。
5. 何らかの記録に違いない。

Unit 6 試練は続く

I. Pre-Viewing

CD 21

A Words

Choose the appropriate word from the list below.

1. Don't think I didn't (   ) you just changed the subject.
2. I'm sorry I (   ) up the box of snakes.
3. I am (   ) this cable right near the hock.
4. It's good for the tigers to feel like they're (   ) for their food like they do in the wild.
5. I did not (   ) the way he kicked the garter snake.
6. A pop by is, by its very (   ), a surprise.
7. Actually quite a lot's been written about the (   ) design of these enclosures.
8. He had a recent bout with kidney disease. That's in (   ) now.
9. The endgame on a big cat can be very (   ).
10. That is the (   ) of a quitting man.

appreciate	costly	definition	innovative	messed
notice	remission	searching	stringing	posture

B Phrases

Study the following phrases.

1. I noticed that your kid really pushes your buttons.
2. You give him a lot of rope.
3. A minute ago, he was into paper airplanes, and now he's into portraits of decapitations.
4. I expected you to be heading for the hills by now.
5. I just can't get a handle on it.

Notes

Goldfish: スイス産のお菓子、クラッカー　**garter snake**: ガーターヘビ
Mayday: an international radio distress signal used by ships and aircraft
hip dysplasia: 股関節形成異常症
buck: dollar（100ドルを表すこともある。例えば、a buck-fifty = $150）

前夜、ディランは届いたばかりの箱の中の大量のヘビに驚いて箱をきちんと閉じていませんでした。登校の準備をしながら口論をするベンジャミンとディラン。さて外に出てみると、庭中に逃げ出したヘビが!　朝から大騒動です。

II. First Viewing

Watch the film and decide if each statement is true (T) or false(F). If you choose F, explain what is wrong.

1. Benjamin is happy to drive Dylan 40,000 miles to school. ( )
2. It was Dylan who messed up the box of snakes. ( )
3. Kelly appreciates what Dylan did with the garter snake. ( )
4. Kelly expects Benjamin to give up managing the zoo and leave there. And he did as she expected. ( )
5. Walter Ferris comes unexpectedly before the actual inspection. ( )
6. Walter Ferris has built a good relationship with MacCready. ( )
7. Benjamin has drawn up an end of life plan for Spar. ( )
8. Walter Ferris gives them 12 top-priority items and two medium-priority items to be done in a month. ( )

III. Second Viewing

Watch the film again and write the name of the speaker (Benjamin, Dylan, Rosie, Kelly, Ferris, Robin). Then watch the film again and put the sentences into the right order.

• Section 1

1. I'll call Kelly. This one seems really not happy with me. (   )[ ]
2. There's nothing you could say to me that's more harsh than what I'm saying to myself. (   )[ ]
3. You're funny with everyone else, but never with me, which I find funny. (   )[ ]

4. I'm pretty sure this is none of my business, but I noticed that your kid really pushes your buttons. (　　　　　　)[　]

5. You're not supposed to say that in this century. (　　　　　　)[　]

6. I'm trying to figure it out. There's no manual for what happened. (　　　　　　)[　]

• Section 2

1. I guess I just don't understand how you can call this place home. (　　　　　　)[　]

2. Look, just be yourself. This is life or death, man. (　　　　　　)[　]

3. You know, actually quite a lot's been written about the innovative design of these enclosures built by Peter MacCready. (　　　　　　)[　]

4. Our inspection happens a week before we open, according to my information. (　　　　　　)[　]

5. He just got here and he's already thinking of quitting. (　　　　　　)[　]

Ⅳ. Dictation

Listen to the CD and fill in the blanks.

Kelly: Now ①______________ here that I am stringing this cable right near the hock, right near the center. So I'm gonna have you string up this carcass ②______________ . It's good for the tigers to feel like they're searching for their food like they do ③______________ .

Benjamin: ④______________ .

Kelly: Hey, I'm pretty sure this is none of ⑤______________, but I noticed that your kid really pushes your buttons. You give him a lot of rope. I did not ⑥______________ the way he kicked that garter snake.

Benjamin: Hey, wait, I ⑦______________ I should be helping you here.

Kelly: It's all good.

Benjamin: Yeah, look, he's 14, and he went through something that no kid should ever have to go through, so I'm giving him a little bit of leeway. Look, honestly, I don't know. I'm trying to ⑧______________ . There's no manual for ⑨______________ . I mean, a minute ago, he was into paper airplanes, and now he's into portraits of decapitations. And they're really good.

Kelly: Yeah, well, what do I know? I ⑩______________ my mother. I'm not good with people.

Listening Tip ◆「濁った th の音」がナ行の子音のように聞こえる

[n] で終わる単語の後に、「ザ」に聞こえる濁った th の音（発音記号は [ð]）で始まる単語が続くと、[n] と th の音がつながって日本語のナ行の子音のように聞こえる事があります。

（例）

1. In the night [インナ].
2. Put your clothes in there [インネア].

V. Post-Viewing

物語の前半が終了しました。ベンジャミンが抱えている問題を整理してみましょう。そして、どのような解決策があるか考えてみましょう。

____

____

____

____

____

____

____

コ・ラ・ム 「ボブ・ディラン」

ベンジャミンが次々と小切手を切りながら奮闘する姿とリリーがディランにサンドイッチを届ける様子が映されるシーン (Unit 5) のバックに流れていた曲は、ボブ・ディランの " Buckets of Rain " である。この曲は、アルバム *Blood on the Tracks* (1975) のラストに収録されている曲で、始まりの " Buckets of rain / Buckets of tears "、そして曲中の " Life is sad / Life is bust " というフレーズは、まさに今のベンジャミンの状況そのものを表しているといえる。ベンジャミンはこの試練をいかに乗り越えるか。ディランは " All ya can do is do what you must do / You do what you must do and ya do well " と歌っている。

「ボブ・ディラン」の名は、この映画ではディランとリリーが屋根の上で星空を眺める場面 (Unit 7) で言及される。リリーはディランに「名前はボブ・ディランからなのね」と呟く。ディランに密かに想いを寄せる彼女にとって、その名前は特別な響きを持つようだ。

では、そのボブ・ディランの名前の由来はというと…彼の本名は、ロバート・アレン・ジマーマン (Robert Allen Zimmerman)。ボブはロバートの愛称。ディランはウェールズの詩人ディラン・トマス (Dylan Thomas, 1914-1953) にちなんで付けられたと言われている。しかし、『自伝』(*Chronicles Volume One*, 2004) によると、当初は「ロバート・アレン」を芸名にするつもりだったようだ。その響きが好きで、自分のアイデンティティはその名にあると感じていたからだそうだ。その頃、偶然ディラン・トマスの詩を読んだ彼は、ディランもいいと悩む。「ロバート・アレン」か「ロバート・ディラン」か。普段の呼称から「ボビー・ディラン」も考えた。さんざん迷ったようだが、フォーク・シンガーとして活動を始める際に名前を訊かれたとき、なぜか本能的に「ボブ・ディラン」と答えていたらしい。

Reading Recess 1

Family Business by the Loved One: *We Bought a Zoo*: Film & Book

It is true that the film is based on an actual story, but the gap between the two is larger than expected. The setting is in California, USA in the film version, while the real story happens in The Dartmoor Zoo in Devon, UK.

Both revolve around, as it were, the family business. But again, there are differences: in the film main characters are Benjamin, his children Dylan (14 years) and Rosie (7 years) as well as Benjamin's older brother Duncan. Involved with them are Kelly and Lily, the former who is an expert zoo worker stands by Benjamin as a kind of a friend and a love combined. Similarly, the latter acts as a romantic friend of Dylan's who is sometimes overwhelmed by a lonely rural life and antipathy against his father. The fact that both children are a little older than their counterparts in the book may be because by so modifying the original the film maker wanted to depict two love stories happening in both adult and juvenile worlds in the Benjamin household.

By contrast, the family business in the book was initiated by Benjamin's old mother and his brother Duncan who already has some experience in zoo management. Benjamin's wife Katherine dies not before the actual story begins like the film but after she has done her bit in helping her husband pave the way to the opening of the zoo. The way husband and wife struggle together against her cancer is dramatically written in the book. The children Milo (6) and Ella (4) are much younger but they try to encourage their father when he is deep in trouble in their own ways. There is no romantic plot besides the moving one between Benjamin and Katherine.

Of course, similarities are abundant. Peter Wearden's case, for example, is a typical example. Wearden is an officer in charge of issuing the zoo license. One of the zoo staff hates him so much that he puts Wearden's picture on the lid of a coffin (book) or on the bull's eye in a darts game at the bar (film).

The fear Benjamin feels towards the roaring lion through the wire is vividly described in both media. The feeling is expressed like this in the book:

"—suddenly he roared and lunged at the wire and I instantly leaped backwards three feet into unknown darkness and brambles. It's impossible to remain impassive in the face of a charging lion. There's something in our primitive mid-brain which tells us it's just not right to be that close to something which can eat us, and the amount of adrenaline dumped into your system at such times is truly primeval."

Both book and film tell us the anguish of those in the zoo when they have no choice but shoot an old and ailing lion, or when they exhaust themselves shouting to frighten a jaguar back into its den. At one time the staff get so weary that they wonder if they should follow Benjamin in what appears to be a futile effort to remodel a dilapidated zoo without aid from the outside, In fact both in film and book they have a meeting to make their angry and frustrated voices heard.

Needless to say, they overcome difficulties, mostly due to the professional work of each member. It is more from the book that we know the details of the professional work each member performs to make the dream come true. Even Kelly is not just a tough zoo keeper like the one played by Scarlet Johansson but a specialist with expertise as well as good connections which help Benjamin gather brilliant staff members from many quarters.

The book also tells us such interesting episodes as meticulous dental care for the animals which requires great manpower and time, difficulties of procuring eating facilities and catering service for the visitors, and, surprisingly, homosexuality found not infrequently among animals.

What merits particular mention is the relation between Benjamin and Katherine in the real story. During their pastoral life in France she is diagnosed with cancer. Since then the life for Benjamin and Katherine has been one of fighting the disease, while raising their children as well as working for the zoo and animals. Benjamin spares no time asking for any medical advice and any promising treatment. In the final stage he gets a palliative and draws up a chart of doses in a desperate attempt to look for a sign of improvement. Even then he candidly reveals their secret:

"Despite everything, the time spent so closely with Katherine was enormously rewarding. She was largely constipated by the steroids, which meant long and fruitless sessions on the toilet. By the time the poo actually exited Katherine, it was so dense and turgid that it wouldn't flush. So we had the poo stick, specially sourced and cut to shape for the breaking up poo into flushable sections. We giggled conspiratorially through these sorts of things, and as we stashed the poo stick (thoroughly cleaned obviously) for future use where no one would find it."

He confesses he is writing this to enhance her memory, believing she is laughing with absolute dignity in a difficult and frightening situation, a laudable attitude and an encouragement for other people going through similarly trying experiences.

Soon after this passage we are told Katherine died.

Notes

revolve around = to focus or center on
a friend and a love combined = both a friend and a love(r), taken as a whole
antipathy = an instinctive opposition in feeling ⇔ sympathy
counterpart = a person resembling in function
do one's bit = to contribute one's share to an effort
pave the way = to prepare, lead up to
bull's eye = the circular spot at the center of a target
primeval = of the first age of the world
futile = incapable of producing any result
dilapidated = reduced into partial ruin or decay
meticulous = taking extreme care about minute details
palliative = something to relieve or lessen pain without curing
constipate = to cause a condition in which feces are too dry and hard to be evacuated
poo = pooh = poop excrement
laudable = deserving praise

EXERCISE

Decide if each sentence is true(T) or false (F).

1. The story takes place in a small American town both in book and film. (   )

2. Dylan was first rebellious against his father for his opposition to the choice of Dylan's girlfriend. (   )

3. Nobody in the family has any experience in zoo management. (   )

4. The time of death of Katherine is different between book and film versions. (   )

5. Peter Wearden is so sympathetic towards Benjamin and his colleagues that they all like him very much. (   )

6. It is one of those ingrained feelings from ancient times that it's just not right to be close to dangerous big animals. (   )

7. The staff have been always obedient to Benjamin and his decisions. (   )

8. Kelly is actually a professional and a specialist in the field of zoo management. (   )

9. In the book more light is shed over the struggle of fighting Katherine's cancer. (   )

10. Benjamin reveals their secret in the book just to make the story funnier. (   )

Unit 7 希望の光

I. Pre-Viewing

CD 25

A Words

Choose the appropriate word from the list below.

1. We can't handle the publicity of an escape! It'll (   ) us.
2. He's been hit by a powerful (   )!
3. Benjamin (   ) him, so he's fine.
4. They're (   ), and they sound like people laughing in the distance.
5. He's like this (   ) creature from the city.
6. I want you to know that I think you're (   ) pretty.
7. The zoo account is empty. I am warning you now. Benjamin Mee is a (   )!
8. She left a (   ) slip. She calls it your circus money.
9. This next part of the letter is kind of (   ). But don't be offended.
10. If you won't listen to your brother, the accountant, then listen to your wife who clearly planned a (   ) future for you.

contained	deposit	exotic	financial	fraud
hurtful	incredibly	primates	ruin	tranquilizer

Phrases

Study the following phrases.

1. I love that you were named after Bob Dylan.
2. No, it's gonna be the other way around.
3. It's a lot to take on.
4. He is going to end up selling this place to somebody for cheap.
5. We'll cut a few corners, but I know we can make the inspection.

Notes

Bob Dylan (1941-): 米国・ミネソタ州出身のミュージシャン。2016 年ノーベル文学賞を受賞
lemur: キツネザル

ベンジャミンがディランを学校に迎えに行った帰り道、脱走したバスターに遭遇します。無事に動物園に連れ戻せるのでしょうか。一方、資金難の動物園に思わぬ救いの手が。

Ⅱ. First Viewing

Watch the film and decide if each statement is true (T) or false(F). If you choose F, explain what is wrong.

1. Benjamin gets Dylan home sick from his school. ( )
2. Buster escapes from the zoo and Benjamin shoots him with a big gun. ( )
3. The veterinarian says Buster will be all right. ( )
4. Kelly is worried Lily is going to hurt Dylan. ( )
5. According to Rhonda, Benjamin is going to sell the zoo for cheap as he has no money. ( )
6. Benjamin gets $84,000 as his wife had a deposit for him. ( )
7. Duncan tries to persuade Benjamin to stay and use the money for the zoo. ( )
8. Dylan feels sorry to hear he may not stay here much longer. ( )

Ⅲ. Second Viewing

Watch the film again and complete the conversation in your own words.

• Section 1

Benjamin → Buster

Hey, Buster. ______________________

____

____

____

____

• Section 2

Kelly → Benjamin

I'm guessing that Rosie was more like your wife and ______________________________

____

____

______________________________.

• Section 3

Duncan ⟷ Benjamin

Duncan: This next part's kind of hurtful.

Benjamin: Yeah.

Duncan: It says "______________________________

____

______________________________."

Benjamin: I know. I read that. She loved you, man.

Lily ⟷ Dylan

Lily: But if you still want to be friends,

____

____

____

______________________________.

Dylan: Well, yeah, of course, but __________

____

____

______________________________.

Ⅳ. Dictation

Listen to the CD and fill in the blanks.

Duncan: This is your cushion. ①______________, man.

Benjamin: Oh, my God.

Duncan: ①______________. It's unbelievable. She's still ②______________ for you, man. She calls it your circus money.

Benjamin: Circus money, yeah.

Duncan: This next part's ③______________.

Benjamin: Yeah.

Duncan: It says, " Listen to your heart, ④______________. "

Benjamin: I know, I ⑤______________. She loved you, man.

Duncan: She ⑥______________ three exclamation marks.

Benjamin: She loved you.

Duncan: Well, I ⑦______________ why you still carry the torch.

Benjamin: Yeah, but with ①______________, we'll cut a few corners, but I know we can make the inspection.

Duncan: No, Benji. Here's what ⑧______________. You're free. You realize that. Listen. Benji. You did it, man. You went to the circus. You changed Dylan and Rosie's lives. They're gonna have those memories forever. But ⑨______________ and ⑩______________ in flames, that's not what Katherine wanted. She wanted you to be free. This money is your ticket out. And if you won't listen to your brother, the accountant, then listen to your wife who clearly planned a financial future for you.

Benjamin: Okay.

Listening Tip ◆ 動名詞、現在分詞の ing は「イング」と言ってない

動名詞や現在分詞の語尾にある ing を「イング」と発音していませんか。今までの dictation の中にあった現在分詞をよく聞いてみてください。「グ」は聞こえなくて「イン」になってますよね。実は ng の綴りは一つの音を表していて発音する際には、「ン」と言わずに、「グ」を口の形だけをして「ン」のように鼻から音を出しているのです。日本語で「四階」と言うときの「ン」がこの音と同じ、舌の後ろを上顎につくくらいまで持ちあげて言う「ン」なのです。

（例）

1.A parking lot [パーキン].

「グ」の音を発音する準備で止めているので、後ろに母音が来ると「グ」の音が聞こえます。

2.I saw her singing [シンギン].

V. Post-Viewing

Dictation で引用された箇所の最後のダンカンの台詞を読んで、ダンカンがどのようにベンジャミンを説得しようとしているかをまとめてみましょう。ダンカンの意見について、あなたはどう思いますか。ベンジャミンはどのような行動をとると思いますか。

____

____

____

____

____

Unit 8「世界一の仕事」に向かって

I. Pre-Viewing

A Words

Choose the appropriate word from the list below.

1. I want to say it has been an (　　　　　　　　) experience here.
2. The financial (　　　　　　　　) being what it is, I think none of us thought we'd come through.
3. I've been an adventure (　　　　　　　　) my whole life, with no regard for cost.
4. Basically, I was just an (　　　　　　　　) and a writer.
5. I just want to say that it's been the best adventure of all because it's (　　　　　　　　).
6. I will need everything from you and we are going to (　　　　　　　　) this zoo.
7. It's really well (　　　　　　　　). It might not work.
8. I work at "Rosemoor Animal Park," and I also (　　　　　　　　) it.
9. You (　　　　　　　　) me nine tickets, 'cause I'm gonna bring the in-laws.
10. If you don't eat the food and you don't get medicine, it all goes (　　　　　　　　) very fast.

addict	amazing	climate	downhill	observer
own	personal	reopen	reserve	worn

B Phrases

Study the following phrases.

1. She's leaving for some job in Mexico and she just turned everybody against you.
2. I do have enough to get us by.
3. If you stick with me, I will give this everything.
4. Don't give up on our adventure.
5. Okay. $74.39. I don't come up with the prices.

Notes

neurotransmitter: 神経伝達物質
El Cajon: a city in southwestern California, east of San Diego

思わず手にしたキャサリンからの「冒険資金」。ベンジャミンはそれを何に使うつもりなのでしょうか。動物園に戻ったベンジャミンは集まっているスタッフに彼の決意を語ります。

II. First Viewing

Watch the film and decide if each statement is true (T) or false(F). If you choose F, explain what is wrong.

1. Benjamin has decided to use Katherine's money to reopen the zoo. ( )
2. Benjamin is certain that he has started his first real adventure. ( )
3. Benjamin tells everybody not to give up on their adventure. ( )
4. Duncan believes Benjamin's decision is what he meant. ( )
5. The cashier is irritated because Benjamin's credit card is not valid. ( )
6. The cashier used to go to the zoo and is looking forward to going there again. ( )
7. The zoo is going to open on July 7. ( )
8. Benjamin is reluctant to let Spar eat the food and get medicine. ( )

III. Second Viewing

Watch the film again and explain the meaning and the situation of these lines in Japanese.

1. Benjamin: This is my first real adventure. And I just want to say that it's been the best one of all because it's personal.

____

____

____

____

2. Rhonda: I don't speak Spanish.

___

___

3. Rosie: How come you don't tell stories anymore?

Benjamin: Well, because we're living the story.

___

___

___

4. Benjamin: It... It'll work.

Cashier: No, no, no. It's just that it says "Rosemoor Animal Park."

___

___

___

___

___

5. Benjamin: You'll be dating seven-year-olds.

___

___

___

IV. Dictation

Listen to the CD and fill in the blanks.

(Outside the restaurant)

Robin: It's Rhonda. She's leaving for some job in Mexico and she just turned everybody against you. They're all in there. ①＿＿＿＿＿＿＿ don't have any more money, man. She says you're a fraud.

Benjamin: I got it.

(In front of the staff)

Benjamin: Well... I want to say it has been ②＿＿＿＿＿＿＿ here. Each of you, I've come to know in some small way. But the financial climate being what it is, I think none of us thought we'd... Well... I don't know how to say this... I've been an adventure addict my whole life. With no big regard for cost. With... Well, with no regard for cost. Basically, I was just ③＿＿＿＿＿＿＿ and a writer. But this is my first real adventure. And I just want to say that it's been the best one of all because ④＿＿＿＿＿＿＿ ... And ⑤＿＿＿＿＿＿＿ my Katherine, the money came through. So, I don't know what you've heard, but I am ⑥＿＿＿＿＿＿＿, though I don't have a lot, I do have enough to get us by. And if you stick with me, I will give this everything. But I will need everything from you and we are going to reopen this zoo. It is ⑦＿＿＿＿＿＿＿ in the world. And it's gonna take everything to make it work. So don't... ⑧＿＿＿＿＿＿＿ on our adventure.

Kelly: Well, that's good enough for me.

Lily: Me, too.

Robin: Done, man.

Benjamin: Circus money, man. Our adventure is just beginning.

Duncan: That's not what I meant.

Benjamin: I know. And Rhonda? I ⑨＿＿＿＿＿＿＿ the best in Mexico.

Rhonda: ⑩＿＿＿＿＿＿＿ Spanish.

Benjamin: Adios.

Listening Tip◆[y] で始まる単語が前の単語にくっついてしまい別の単語に聞こえる

単語の先頭の [y] 音は前の単語の一番後ろの子音とくっつきます。英語話者にとって新しい音になっているわけではないのですが、日本語の拗音（小さい「ャ」「ュ」「ョ」をつけて書く音）に聞こえてしまうことで、[y] の前にある単語が違う単語に聞こえてしまったり、[y] で始まる単語を聞き落としてしまったりします。特に代名詞 you は強く発音されることが少ないためしばしば動詞や前置詞の後ろでこの変化を起こして聞こえなくなります。

（例）

1. Thank you [サンキュー] very much.
2. Could you [クッヂュ] send it directly to me?
3. I am going to visit the USJ this year [ディシァ].

V. Post-Viewing

もしあなたが思わぬ「冒険資金」を手にしたら、どのように使いますか。次の質問の答えになるように、続きの文章を作ってみましょう。

Q: If you got the circus money, what would you do with the money?

A: If I got the circus money, I would ________________________________.

Unit 9 死を受け入れる時期

I. Pre-Viewing

A Words

Choose the appropriate word from the list below.

1. He got up there and can't come down. We tried (   ) him with food.
2. He's slow, I can (   ) him.
3. Loud noises (   ) the big cats.
4. You just (   ), scream, and make as much noise as possible.
5. Benjamin tried to drag Spar out by himself because he was (   ).
6. He's suffering and in a lot of pain. I can't (   ) watching it.
7. You can't see how (   ) this is to extend his life.
8. Get him some medicine and (   ) in a little bit of hope!
9. Dad will be back soon. He's just having a (   ).
10. Her favorite bushes grew flowers all over our neighborhood. They're all (   ) to remember our happy days.

desperate	invest	luring	mood	outrun
scare	selfish	stand	triggers	yell

Phrases

Study the following phrases.

1. Do you think I want to come out here and drag you out here?
2. Like, maybe we're all a bit in each other's pockets.
3. No, I can't stand by and watch this happen!
4. Well, it's not up to you.
5. Just can't get a handle on it. I cannot let go.

Notes

Home Depot: ホームデポ、家庭用品販売チェーンストア
Pop-Tarts: ポップターツ、米国のペストリー

動物園の再開に向けて奮闘するベンジャミンですが、キャサリンのことではまだ心の整理がつかず、思い出の写真のファイルを開くこともできませんでした。さて、そんなある日、スパーが大変なことに! いったい何が起こったのでしょう。

II. First Viewing

Watch the film and decide if each statement is true (T) or false(F). If you choose F, explain what is wrong.

1. Spar cannot come down from the rock because he is stuck. ( )
2. Loud noises do not affect Spar. ( )
3. It is unbearable for Kelly to see Spar in a lot of pain. She knows he is going to die. ( )
4. Kelly thinks it is selfish of man to extend Spar's life and Benjamin agrees. ( )
5. Dylan says Benjamin has had a mood for a couple years. ( )
6. Dylan does not like girls because they talk too much. ( )
7. It is easy for Benjamin not to think about his wife, as nothing reminds him of her in the zoo. ( )
8. It is hard for Benjamin to see his wife's eyes in Dylan's eyes. ( )

III. Second Viewing

Watch the film again and summarize the situation.

• A

The problem: Spar got up on the rock and ____________________.

His situation: He has got to ______________, ________________ and take ________________.

He has ____________________.

What each person tries or suggests to do:

Benjamin: He ____.

Robin: "It's time. ______________________________."

Lily: "Loud noises ______________________________."

• B

Kelly's opinion about the problem of Spar:

"He's in a lot of pain. I can't ______________________________.

"He's in so much pain. They can't tell you, but ____________________.

"It's going ______________."

Benjamin's opinion:

"I'm saying, we just let him ______________________________.

Get him some medicine and ______________________________."

Ⅳ. Dictation

CD 35

Listen to the CD and fill in the blanks.

Benjamin: I thought if I came out here ①______________. Back home, every place reminded me of her. Filippe's on Third Street. Balboa Park. Little Dom's, the coffee shop, that... That's a big one. I mean, the air, the way it smelled in May and August, because those were the months that ②______________ bushes grew flowers all over our neighborhood. They're all triggers, man. And it got better for a while. I mean, it... It did, out here. But the funny thing is that it just turns out that she's here, too. I mean, I go to Home Depot. I go to the nine-miles-away Target.

Kelly: We ③______________.

Benjamin: And seriously, I'm avoiding half the aisles. Condiments. Pastries, ④______________. She loved red kites and blueberry Pop-Tarts. I mean, who doesn't, right?

Kelly: Who doesn't?

Benjamin: If only I could talk to her about ⑤______________.

Kelly: Yeah.

Benjamin: And most of all, it's the kids. They're the biggest triggers of all. I mean, Dylan. His eyes. You know, I've only seen ⑥______________ in somebody's eyes once in my life. And the way he just drives me nuts, he makes me crazy. Denies me, ⑦______________ me. And all the time, he's looking back at me with her eyes. And none of her lightness. What I've figured out is that when you love somebody that much, that hard, that long, you can never get away from them, ⑨______________ you go. And that only comes once ⑧______________. Just can't get a handle on it. I cannot let go.

Kelly: I can. Sleep well, Benjamin. ⑩______________.

CD 36

Listening Tip ◆二つの母音に挟まれた [t] がラ行の子音に聞こえる

単語の中に「母音 + [t] + 弱い母音」または「母音 + [t] +「オー」のように聞こえる [l]」という音の連続がある場合は、[t] は日本語のラ行の音に聞こえます。

（例）

1. water [ワラー]
2. party [パーリー]
3. Whatever [ワレバー].

しかし、逆に後ろの母音にアクセントが置かれるとこの変化は起きません。

4. protest [プロテスト](注：動詞です)

また、「母音 + [t]」で終わる単語の後に母音で始まる単語が切れ目なく発音される時にも同じように [t] はラ行の音になります。(この場合は後ろに来る母音にアクセントがあってもかまいません。)

5. Get out of it [ゲラウロブイッ].

V. Post-Viewing

Dictation で引用されている箇所を読んで、ベンジャミンの今の心境をまとめてみましょう。映画の場面ではこの会話をディランが聴いていますが、ディランはどのような気持ちでいると思いますか。次の場面も予測してみましょう。

Unit 10 家族の絆を取り戻そう

I. Pre-Viewing

A Words

Choose the appropriate word from the list below.

1. " You hate me. " " I hate you? Wait a ( ). "
2. It's your dream! You can't ( ) a dream onto someone else.
3. The line of people in this world who really care about you ( ) here!
4. It's like you ( ) yourself if you say something.
5. All you need is 20 seconds of courage, ( ) 20 seconds of bravery.
6. That looks good. You are in your ( ).
7. Dad? Dad, the peacocks are ( )!
8. I saw an iguana and ( ) Indian in my dream.
9. Duncan, you're scattering fallen leaves. That ( ) its own purpose!
10. It is ( ) that I looked worse than him.

defeats	dwarf	embarrass	ends	force
hatching	humiliating	literally	prime	second

B Phrases

Study the following phrases.

1. We've had problems, but we're <u>figuring it out</u>, okay?
2. <u>Hold on</u>! Enough with the drama!

3. Knock it off! You misheard me!

4. Stop moping around this place! Do something!

5. My brother can't take no for answer.

Notes

bullshit: stupid or untrue talk or writing
Easter Bunny: 復活祭のウサギ（復活祭に贈り物を持ってくるといわれる）
tranq gun: 麻酔銃（tranq<tranquilizer）
haddock: タラ　　　***Altered States***: 映画「未知への挑戦」

すれ違いぶつかり合う父と子。妻を、母を失い、バラバラになりかけた家族の絆が、死を迎えた一頭のトラを通して再びつながっていきます。

II. First Viewing

Watch the film and decide if each statement is true (T) or false(F). If you choose F, explain what is wrong.

1. Dylan thinks that Benjamin hates him.　　(　　)

2. Benjamin is not aware of that Dylan needs his father's help. ( )
3. Dylan confesses that he doesn't like Lily so much. ( )
4. Benjamin still can't see pictures of his dead wife and the family. ( )
5. Benjamin uses Dylan's drawing for the poster of the zoo. ( )
6. Duncan comes to the zoo to persuade Benjamin to quit the zoo. ( )
7. Benjamin nails the small plaque to the lion enclosure. ( )
8. Staffs raise the new sign for the front of the zoo. ( )

III. Second Viewing

Watch the film again, then summarize how Benjamin came to overcome difficulties in his relationships with the people around him.

• Section 1

At their home	Benjamin quarrels with his son, Dylan.

• Section 2

In the tiger enclosure	Benjamin talks with Dylan in front of Spar's cage.

• Section 3

In the kitchen	Benjamin can see photos of his dead wife and the family.

• Section 4

In the zoo office	Benjamin shows the poster.

• Section 5

In the yard in front of the house	Duncan comes by his car.

Ⅳ. Dictation

Listen to the CD and fill in the blanks.

Benjamin: Hey, I need you ①_______________. I gotta...

Dylan: Sure...

Benjamin: borrow your artist's eye. You gotta tell me ②_______________...
about this. Not bad? Huh?

Dylan: ③_______________ this?

Benjamin: I don't know. I was thinking maybe everywhere. I'm your fan, man. Don't you know that by now?

Rosie: Dad? Dad, the peacocks are hatching!

Benjamin: ④______________ all names, Rosie?

Rosie: Mmm-hmm.

Dylan: Which one's that one ⑤______________ ?

Rosie: Lucy. Wait, not Lucy. Peaches.

Benjamin: Peaches. How do you ⑥______________ all straight? You have three named Peaches.

Benjamin: Would somebody just get my tranq gun? My brother can't take no for an answer.

Duncan: Not why I'm here, bro. I talked to MacCready. Hello, children. I ⑦______________ if you guys needed any help. In the trunk of this car is haddock. Two hundred pounds' worth. For Bruno.

Benjamin: Buster.

Duncan: Whatever.

Benjamin: Are you serious?

Duncan: No. Serious is ⑧______________. I started questioning my entire being back there ⑨______________. It was like Altered States. I saw an iguana and a dwarf Indian.

Benjamin: Aw, Dunc.

Duncan: All right. Come on. Got ⑩______________ tomorrow.

Benjamin: So we do.

Duncan: So we do.

Listening Tip◆動詞や前置詞の後のthemは「ザ」が脱落して「エム」になる

強く読まれることが少ない代名詞themは前の単語と連続すると先頭の「ゼ」が発音されなくなります。家族や友達のように親しい者への愛情を表す言い方です。

（例）

1. Get them [ゲッエム].
2. You say, you ate them [エイッエム] up?

V. Post-Viewing

映画の中に出てくるたとえについて考えてみましょう。

1. Like you were talking about cornflakes.
2. a seven-year-old girl who still believes in the Easter Bunny.
3. It was like *Altered States*. I saw an iguana and dwarf Indian.

このユニット以外にもたとえを使った表現が色々出てきます。探してみましょう。

コ・ラ・ム 「原題 vs 邦題」

本作の原題は *We Bought a Zoo* だ。直訳すると『動物園買っちゃった』となる。それを『幸せへのキセキ』とするのは全くの意訳である。「キセキ」とカタカナ表記してあるのは「奇跡」と「軌跡」を掛け合わせたつもりだろうか。意訳なら『ファミリー動物園』でも『家族で動物園経営』でもいいのだが、はたしてこの邦題の出来は如何。

映画の原題と邦題の関係にはいくつかのパタンがある。まず、英語をそのままカタカナにした安易というか、むしろストレートでインパクトがあると言うべきやり方がある。『サウンド・オブ・ミュージック』(1965)、『ジョーズ』(1975)、『タイタニック』(1997)、『アバター』(2009)、『ジュラシック・ワールド』(2015)、『ブラック・パンサー』(2018)、あるいはマーベルものなど最近のアクションものはその傾向が強いようだ。むろん、直訳の日本語を邦題にしたもの、たとえば、『真夜中のカウボーイ』(*Midnight Cowboy*, 1969)、『大脱走』(*The Great Escape*, 1963) も同類である。

次に原題とつかず離れず型ともいうべき手法。たとえば、『アパートの鍵貸します』(1960) の原題は *The Apartment*、一歩作品に踏み込んだ訳である。『野生のエルザ』(1966) はどうだろうか。原題 *Born Free* を生かしつつ主役のライオンの名を入れて具体化している。『卒業』(1967) の原題は *The Graduate*「卒業生」だ。どちらが印象的なのか。『危険な情事』(1987) と原題 *Fatal Attraction* の優劣の判定も難しい。『ゼロ・グラビティ』対 *Gravity* も微妙だ。ストーリー展開と言葉の印象が関わり判断に迷いそうである。問題含みの例をひとつあげておくと、1979 年の『クレーマー、クレーマー』だ。原題は *Kramer vs Kramer* で、アメリカの裁判で使われる対立図式がベースになっていて、子供の養育権を巡る (Mr.)Kramer 対 (vs)(Mrs.)Kramer という意味ある表題なのだが、邦題だと、名前が連呼されるだけの間の抜けたタイトルになっている。

本作同様の自由な邦題となると枚挙にいとまがない。『わが心のボルティモア』(*Avalon*,1960)、『俺たちに明日はない』(*Bonnie and Clyde*, 1967)、『明日に向かって撃て!』(*Butch Cassidy and Sundance Kid*, 1969)、『狼よさらば』(*Death Wish*, 1974)、『愛と青春の旅立ち』(*An Officer and a Gentleman*, 1982)、『天使にラブソングを』(*Sister Act*,1992)、『海の上のピアニスト』(*The Legend of 1900*, 1998)、『裏切りのサーカス』(*Tinker Tailor Soldier Spy*,2011)、『オデッセイ』(*The Martian*, 2015) などなど。大ヒットした『アナと雪の女王』も原題は *Frozen*。たしかに原題のままだとヨーグルトかアイスクリームの話と勘違いされかねないから、親切な邦題というべきかもしれない。

Unit 11 検査の通過は？

I. Pre-Viewing

A Words

Choose the appropriate word from the list below.

1. To be (   ), sir, it always was adventure.
2. "How are you?" "On my best (   )."
3. You asked me (   ), so I came here.
4. The only way to (   ) the lock is to jimmy it from the inside.
5. I'm going to (   ) him from the other side of this enclosure.
6. I'm filled with Scotch and bitterness and (   ) thoughts!
7. I don't (   ), Mr. Mee. I'm sure I'll have plenty of bad reports.
8. The (   ) tonight is just a hint of what's yet to come this summer.
9. I would (   ) put this on your summer to do list: get an umbrella.
10. Can you check on the (   ) order?

behavior	definitely	distract	fix	fraternize
impure	invoice	politely	precipitation	precise

Phrases

Study the following phrases.

1. All right, here we go.
2. You're never that polite. What's up?
3. I can only keep his attention for so long!
4. What happens if literally we did this whole thing for nothing?
5. "I was named after a dog named Dylan." "I don't even care. Who cares?"

Notes

walkies: walky-talky トランシーバー
jimmy(v) : force open with a jimmy（「かなとこ」）
Sheep farts in aspic!: ののしり言葉　aspic は「肉や魚の煮汁にゼラチンや調味料を加えて作るゼリー」のこと
Scotch: Scotch whisky
dick: stupid or contemptible person（もとは police officer, inspector, detective などの意味）
lion: a brave, strong, or fierce person

運命の検査日。動物園を再開するにはこの検査に通らなくてはなりません。結果は果たして? 天はベンジャミンたちに味方してくれるのでしょうか。

II. First Viewing

Watch the film and decide if each statement is true (T) or false(F). If you choose F, explain what is wrong.

1. Walter Ferris is the US police officer. ( )
2. Ferris inspects the animals' enclosures roughly. ( )
3. The lock of the lion enclosure is stuck in the open position. ( )
4. The problem of the lion enclosure is solved by Kelly and MacCready. ( )
5. Ferris checks a box, "approved" and the zoo will be able to open on schedule. ( )
6. Dylan and Lily make up and hug each other. ( )
7. Benjamin and Duncan have confidence in the zoo's success. ( )
8. According to the weather forecast, the record storm will continue. ( )

III. Second Viewing

Watch the film again and answer the questions. (1) Write down the process of Ferris's inspection. (2) Explain the weather conditions before the opening day.

(1) Hints: camels, final inspection report, otters, roof, schedule, Solomon, straws, wall

He inspects ______________________________.

______________________________.

______________________________.

______________________________.

______________________________.

______________________________.

______________________________.

He checks ______________________________.

(2) ____

____

____

____

Ⅳ. Dictation

Listen to the CD and fill in the blanks.

Kelly: Thank God you're here. I asked you so politely, I didn't think ①______________.

MacCready: And ②______________. You're never that polite. What's up?

Kelly: ③______________ and I feel like the only way... Oh, God, the only way to fix it is to jimmy it from the inside.

MacCready: ④______________.

Kelly: We're going to fail this inspection.

MacCready: Calm down. We're not gonna fail it. You're going to calm down.

Kelly: Yes, I am.

MacCready: What are you gonna do to help?

Kelly: I'm gonna distract him from the other side of this enclosure and you're gonna not ⑤______________! ... All right, it's gonna be fine... Okay. Hey, hey, Solomon! Who's a handsome boy? Come on, Solomon. Come on, baby! Over here. Ooh! Hey! Solomon! Can you hear me? Come on, Solomon, come on, baby!

Benjamin: Hey, do you want something to drink?

Ferris: I don't drink.

Benjamin: Well, not even water?

Ferris: Do you have any idea what they put in water?

Kelly: Over here. Hey, good boy, good Solomon! Good Solomon! Good boy! Good boy! Who's a good boy? Who's a good boy? Who's a handsome boy? ... ⑥______________! Hurry up! Would you hurry up? I can only keep his attention for so long! Hi, boy! Hi, boy! Fix it, fix it, would you?

MacCready: I like to ⑦______________! ... Sheep farts in aspic! Cocktails!

Kelly: No, no, no, no! Wait! Solomon! Solomon! Come here! Come here! Come here! Come here! Oh, God! Don't turn around. Don't turn around! Turn around. Turn around!

MacCready: You don't want me! I am filled with Scotch and bitterness and impure thoughts!

Kelly: ⑧______________ Ferris ⑨______________ ! MacCready!

MacCready: ⑩______________ !

Listening Tip ◆「母音＋[t]＋弱い母音＋[n]」の [t] と弱い母音が聞こえなくなる

Unit 9 で見た「母音 + [t] + 弱い母音」の後ろに [n] が来ると [t] の音が聞こえなくなります。少し複雑な変化ですが、[t] が口の形だけ (舌先を上の前歯のすぐ後ろの歯茎につける) 作られて破裂しないまま (弱い [n] になる) になり、次に来る弱い母音は脱落して発音されず次の [n] が聞こえます。例では「・ン」と示しましたが、「(ン) ン」のように小さな「ン」が聞こえることもあります。かっこいい発音なので練習してみて下さい。日本語の「ン」をそのまま出すのではなく、[n] の音は舌先を上の前歯のすぐ後ろの歯茎につけて出して発音してください。

(例)

1. button [バッ・ン]
2. gotten [ガーッ・ン]
3. written [リッ・ン]

V. Post-Viewing

次の英文は Ferris 検査官が記入していた用紙に書かれていた英文です。どのようなものか見てみましょう。またこの用紙を記入したときの彼の気持ちはどんなものだったのか、考えてみましょう。

United States Department of Agriculture
Animal and Plant Health Inspection Service
Animal Care

FINAL INSPECTION REPORT

Rosemoor Animal Park Adventure　Site 9087　31-R-0764
SAME

NARRATIVE

SEE INVENTORY SHEET

CATEGORY 1; Compliant item(s) previously identified that have been corrected.
Section 3-3-4©3.3. (b) General Inspection FINAL

The final inspection has been accessed by Inspector Ferris and deemed complete.
All provisions and non-compliant infractions have been corrected to satisfaction.

☐ Denied　☐ Approved

Prepared by　Date 6 / 30/ '10

Unit 12 開園ともう一つの始まりの物語

I. Pre-Viewing

A Words

Choose the appropriate word from the list below.

1. These are French braids. They were ( ) in the '90s.
2. I know that I ( ) at speeches, so I won't even try.
3. I would have taken full ( ) if my wife were here.
4. Anything that happens from here on out is a ( ).
5. "Dad, something is wrong!" "( ), my son. ( )."
6. Would you like a ( ) of this zoo?
7. Peafowl are very ( ) animals.
8. I got a big ( ) on you, Ben.
9. Those words have guided me my ( ) life.
10. This is the moment where both of you became a ( ).

big	bonus	brochure	credit	crush
entire	patience	possibility	resilient	stink

B Phrases

Study the following phrases.

1. Maybe it is supposed to be this way.
2. As you can see, the tigers know that you're here.

3. Today these tigers are very active. They are showing off!

4. If we're standing near each other on New Year's, we'll do this again.

5. I'm going for it. Bravery.

Notes

French braids: 三つ編みの一種	**goofball**: まぬけ

無事再開にこぎつけた動物園ですが、見物客は来てくれるのでしょうか。家族の絆を取り戻したベンジャミンたちは、様々な人たちとさらにつながっていきます。

II. First Viewing

Watch the film and decide if each statement is true (T) or false(F). If you choose F, explain what is wrong.

1. It is fine on the morning of the opening day, July 7th, 2010. (　　)

2. Benjamin is good at speeches, so he makes a long one to the staff. (　　)

3. No one comes to the zoo at opening time because of a traffic accident. ( )

4. The staff help many people who scramble up the fallen tree. ( )

5. Many people visit the zoo, but no one praises Benjamin. ( )

6. Benjamin and Kelly confess their emotions to each other in the ticket kiosk. ( )

7. There are a lot of red kites in the sky. ( )

8. Benjamin cannot tell his children how to meet Katherine. ( )

Ⅲ. Second Viewing

The end of the film, Benjamin tells his children a wonderful story. Watch the film again and summarize the situation how Benjamin and his wife Katherine meet at LITTLE DOM'S Coffee Shop with the help of the hints below.

Hints: seventeen years ago, Benjamin, walk, coffee shop, saw, Katherine, sitting, was stunned, thought, she, the most beautiful woman, he, talked, total stranger, encouraged, 20 seconds courageousness, swept up to, talked, "Excuse me" "Why would an amazing woman like you even talk to someone like me?" "Why not"

____

____

____

____

____

____

____

____

____

____

____

Ⅳ. Dictation

Listen to the CD and fill in the blanks.

Benjamin: Dylan?

Rosie: Dylan! Dad!

Benjamin: Dyl?

Dylan: ①______________.

Benjamin: Okay. Get ready. Whoa! ②______________, turn around. Let me see. What the hair! What happened to the hair?

Kelly: French braids. Big in the '90s.

Benjamin: Nice, very nice.

Kelly: They're gonna be here today, Benjamin. I know it. ③______________, this place'll be packed.

Benjamin: Okay, well, we all know that I stink ④______________ , so I won't even try. If Katherine were here, she would have come up with something really funny and clever for me to say, and I'd have taken ⑤______________. It's not about where an adventure ends, ⑥______________ that's not what an adventure's about. So anything that happens from here on out is a bonus. And I love you guys.

MacCready: Okay! ⑦______________! It's a zoo!

Duncan: Yes, it is!

(Applause)

Rosie: What time is it?
Duncan: ⑧______________.
Dylan: They should be here.
Benjamin: Patience, my son. Patience.
Duncan: No, he's right. They should be here.
Benjamin: Look, maybe it's supposed to be this way. I don't know. Maybe it's supposed to ⑨______________.
Dylan: Dad, something's wrong.
Benjamin: Dylan?
Dylan: No, something's wrong!
Benjamin: Dyl!
(At the fallen trees)
Dylan: The tree fell down ⑩______________! They couldn't have gotten through even if they were here.
(On the top of the trees.)
Benjamin: Welcome! Come on, come on, we're open!

Listening Tip◆弱い母音は聞き取りにくい

早口やくだけた会話の中では、アクセントのつかない母音は口をあまり開けない曖昧母音 [ə] となります。日本人にとってこの音は「ア」「イ」「ウ」「エ」「オ」のどの母音にも聞こえてしまうため、単語の綴りと違う音が聞こえて困る時があります。冠詞の a、the、ほとんどの前置詞の母音は強調しない限りこの [ə] です。and が [エンド] や [ォンド] と聞こえるのはこのためです。例では [ə] を「ォ」として示します。

（例）

1. A [ォ] bird in the [ォナ] hand is worth two in the [ォナ] bush.
   弱い母音を注意せずに力を抜いて発音することでエネルギーを節約しているそうです。しかし、次の場合などは音で区別が出来なくなります。
2. On the [ォナ] first Monday in [ォン] July.
   こうなると in と on の区別は文法に頼るしかありません。

V. Post-Viewing

次の英文は最後にスクリーンに登場するタイトルです。声に出して読んでみましょう。映画の中でこのタイトルが流れていくスピードで読むことができますか。またキリンのエピソードが出てくるのはなぜなのか考えてみましょう。

The Zoological Park, on which this story is based, is an award-winning zoo whose methods are admired around the world. The park is open to faithful followers year-round. Benjamin Mee and his two kids still live on the grounds. Next year, they plan to add giraffes.

Reading Recess 2

Man and Wildlife in Film

Hollywood has a long history of films depicting interaction between people and wild animals. The following three, among others, stand out in their own ways.

Born Free (1966) is a true story based on Joy Adamson's 1960 non-fiction book *Born Free* in which she and her husband George are forced to kill a lion after the lion kills a native Kenya villager. The Adamsons take care of the three orphaned lion cubs and in time the two largest are sent to a zoo in Holland, while Elsa the smallest lioness stays with Joy. When Elsa grows big enough to stampede a herd of elephants, the couple are faced with the choice — releasing her to the wild or sending her to a zoo.

Joy opposes sending Elsa to a zoo and spends much time trying to reintroduce her to the wild in a distant reserve. After a long struggle Joy succeeds in rehabilitating Elsa to the wild, and with heartbreaking feelings she returns Elsa to the wild of Kenya. Joy and George depart for their home in England but a year later they return to Kenya for a short visit, hoping for a reunion with Elsa. Indeed they find Elsa has not forgotten them and that man-animal friendship has taken firm root in a vast expanse of African plain. Moreover, to their happiness Elsa is now a mother of three cubs.

One film critic writes in *The New York Times*, "Without minimizing the facts of animal life or overly sentimentalizing them, this film casts an enchantment that is just about irresistible." *Born Free* was an inspiration for Benjamin Mee. He says in the book that he is grateful to his wife Katherine for encouraging him to go for his dream of running a zoo. In fact he calls his wife 'my Born Free Lady' after the leading actress in the film which is for him "the seminal film" about "Joy and George Adamson rearing and reintroducing Elsa the abandoned lioness back into the wilds of Africa." "That seemed to me like a very good job to have," he confesses.

Gorillas in the Mist (1988) is also a true story, but with a touch of sadness in the ending. A therapist Dian Fossey is inspired by an anthropologist friend to devote her life to the study of primates. She succeeds in getting herself involved in a project in Congo. With the help of an animal tracker she locates a group of gorillas, but unfortunately she is suspected of being a spy and displaced during the Congo Crisis. Then she bases her research efforts in the jungles of neighboring Rwanda where she later finds there are problems of poaching and corruption. Dian makes some discoveries in gorilla's communication and social behavior, thus earning her international attention.

She establishes a close and emotional bond with a male gorilla named Digit and tries to prevent the export of other gorillas. In spite of her repeated complaints the Rwandan government does little to stop appalling poaching of the gorillas for their skin, hands and heads. Dian's anger reaches the limit when her beloved Digit is killed and beheaded by poachers. She begins to take extreme measures such as burning down the poachers' villages and a mock execution of an offender.

Then, we are told quite shockingly that some years later Dian Fossey is found brutally murdered in her own bedroom by an unknown attacker. Her friends attend the funeral in the same cemetery where Digit and other gorillas are buried. They just wish Dian and Digit are happily reunited in heaven at the end. The gorillas are saved from extinction in a way by her brave actions which come out of her affection and friendship for Digit the gorilla.

Free Willy (1993) is a story of friendship between an abandoned lonely boy Jesse and an orca whale taken away from his family. Jesse, a street child, hides himself in a marine theme park. To avoid punishment he has to help out at the aquarium. It is then and there that he meets the gentle orca. Sharing a lonely family history, the boy and the whale form a strong friendship over time.

On account of Jesse's arduous training Willy is to debut for a show, but the excited audience begin to pound on the tank glass, making the scared Willy too panicked to continue the show. Then the theme park president decides to kill Willy for insurance money. Overhearing the plot, Jesse attempts to release Willy into the ocean. Despite the president's persistent disturbances they reach the ocean and Willy, with his excellent jumping, gets over a number of pursuing boats into his family which have come to rescue him.

Family reunion is not just for Willy but Jesse is also finally embraced in the bosom of his step parent. Though different in species, here are two lonely hearts gathered together to help and encourage each other to live for a life of love. The animal actor Keiko which plays Willy's role brilliantly, when returned to an ill-managed Mexican marine park, resumed contact with people and soon died of pneumonia. What a sad irony!

Notes

stand out = to be conspicuous, prominent
stampede = to cause to make a rush
reserve = land set apart for a special purpose
reunion = the act of uniting again
cub = the young of certain animals, as the bear, lion, or tiger
seminal = highly original and influencing the development of future events
touch = slight amount of some quality
primate = any of various mammals
displace = to compel a person to leave home, country
poach = to trespass another's game preserve to steal animals or to hunt
behead = to cut off the head
extinction = to wipe out of existence
arduous = requiring great exertion, very difficult
persistent = constantly repeated, continued
disturbance = interruption, interference which causes trouble
bosom = the breast of a human being
irony = an outcome of events contrary to what was or might have been expected

EXERCISE

次の設問に答えなさい。

1. *Born Free* というタイトルに秘められた意味は何だと考えられるか。

2. 『幸せへのキセキ』 に *Born Free* はどのように 関係しているのか。

3. ダイアンはなぜあのような極端な行動に出たのか。

4. ダイアンの葬儀に参列した人々の願いとは何であったのか。

5. ジェシーとウイリーの共通点は何か。

6. ウイリー役を演じたオルカを襲った皮肉な運命とは。

音声ファイルのダウンロード方法

英宝社ホームページ（http://www.eihosha.co.jp/）の
「テキスト音声ダウンロード」バナーをクリックすると、
音声ファイルダウンロードページにアクセスできます。

We Bought a Zoo
映画『幸せへのキセキ』

2020年2月25日　初　版　　2022年2月10日　2刷

編著者© 森岡裕一
沖野泰子
白木智士
山科美和子
横山三鶴

発行者 佐々木元

発行所 株式会社 英宝社
〒101-0032 東京都千代田区岩本町2-7-7
Tel［03］(5833) 5870　Fax［03］(5833) 5872

ISBN978-4-269-09007-1 C1082
［製版：(株)マナ・コムレード／印刷：モリモト印刷(株)／表紙デザイン：伊谷企画］